CONTEN

CHOICE

Airea D. Matthews • *Bread and Circus* • Picador

RECOMMENDATIONS

Selima Hill • *Women in Comfortable Shoes* • Bloodaxe Books
Lisa Kelly • *The House of the Interpreter* • Carcanet
Majella Kelly • *The Speculations of Country People* • Penguin
Adam Lowe • *Patterflash* • Peepal Tree Press

SPECIAL COMMENDATION

Ed. Shash Trevett, Vidyan Ravinthiran, Seni Seneviratne
• *Out of Sri Lanka Anthology* • Bloodaxe Books

TRANSLATION CHOICE

Alasdair Mac Mhaighstir Alasdair • *Dastram / Delirium*
Translated by Taylor Strickland • Broken Sleep Books

PAMPHLET CHOICE

Karen Downs-Barton • *Didicoy* • Smith / Doorstop

Poetry Book Society

CHOICE SELECTORS RECOMMENDATION SPECIAL COMMENDATION	JO CLEMENT & ROY McFARLANE
TRANSLATION SELECTOR	HARRY JOSEPHINE GILES
PAMPHLET SELECTORS	NINA MINGYA POWLES & ARJI MANUELPILLAI
CONTRIBUTORS	SOPHIE O'NEILL MEGAN ROBSON LEDBURY CRITICS
EDITORIAL & DESIGN	ALICE KATE MULLEN

Poetry Book Society Memberships
Choice
4 Books a Year: 4 Choice books & 4 *Bulletins* (UK £65, Europe £85, ROW £120)
World
8 Books: 4 Choices, 4 Translation books & 4 *Bulletins* (£98, £160, £190)
Complete
24 Books: 4 Choices, 16 Recommendations, 4 Translations & 4 *Bulletins* (£230, £290, £36C

Single copies of the *Bulletin* £9.99

Cover Artwork 'Inner City' by Graeme Hopper @grazzziazzzi

Poetry Book Society | Milburn House | Dean Street | Newcastle upon Tyne | NE1 1LF
0191 230 8100 | enquiries@poetrybooksociety.co.uk
WWW.POETRYBOOKS.CO.UK

LETTER FROM THE PBS

In my last letter I promised more in-person events, and by the time you read this we will have held the Newcastle Poetry Festival. Now in its eighth year, this is a major event in the calendar for fans of international contemporary poetry. The Poetry Book Society is a key partner alongside the poetry publisher Bloodaxe and NCLA at Newcastle University. All of the events were filmed so if you couldn't be there in person you can find them on the NCLA youtube channel, including readings from our Summer Choice, Airea D. Matthews, and recommended poet Adam Lowe.

We are committed to promoting live poetry events and are passionate about attracting poetry readers to discover the beautiful towns and cities, countryside and coastline of the north east. We understand our readers are spread across the country so are, of course, looking to be involved in more national events over the second half of the year and beyond.

I feel this season's *Bulletin* is a lesson in empathy – we readers are treated to an insight into the lived experiences of marginalised people and their communities. Our summer choice is a memoir-in-verse, *Bread and Circus* by Airea D. Matthews who writes, "the book amalgamates spectral imaging, photography, and poetry to explore the social and economic realities of race and class in America" and was born from a study trip to research Adam Smith's *Wealth of Nations*.

I won't talk about all the books – the *Bulletin* is here for you to browse! I just hope you enjoy these recommendations, selections and reviewed titles as much as we have. I hope they find a good home with you, our Poetry Book Society members, and that you'll help to spread the word about all of these brilliant books.

SOPHIE O'NEILL
PBS & INPRESS DIRECTOR

Image: A.H. Jerriod Avant

AIREA D. MATTHEWS

Airea D. Matthews' first collection of poems was the critically acclaimed *Simulacra* which received the prestigious 2016 Yale Series of Younger Poets Award. Her new collection *Bread and Circus* is a memoir-in-verse that explores the realities of economic necessity, marginal poverty and commodification. She received a 2016 Rona Jaffe Foundation Writers' Award, a 2020 Pew Fellowship and was named Philadelphia's Poet Laureate in 2022. Matthews holds a BA in Economics from the University of Pennsylvania as well as an MFA from the Helen Zell Writers' Program and an MPA from the Gerald Ford School of Public Policy, both at the University of Michigan. She is an associate professor at Bryn Mawr College where she co-directs the poetry program.

BREAD AND CIRCUS

PICADOR | £10.99 | PBS PRICE £8.25

Airea D. Matthews' *Bread and Circus* is a revisionist memoir-in-verse about African American poverty. Here, substance dependency looms as large as the injurious economic systems that cause it:

after OPEC raised the price of oil/my father cuffed up the hem of his pants and handed me a needle/for the drug addict to have someone else shoot them up is a sacred intimacy–

Matthews redacts *The Wealth of Nations* to reveal anti-capitalist rally cries, locating what Jean Binta Breeze dubs "a voice, not a page". The many voices in this palimpsest shimmer like KoolAid and rat poison crystals alike. At a now shut-down HIV and AIDS hospital, we overhear deathbed prayers ('Penitence'). A nervous teen manifests the dangers of Black existence, urging his brother to rearrange his public appearance ('Animalia Repeating'). In 'Working-Class Bedtime Story, 1981' a disenfranchised mother unravels before a terrified, neglected child who is left:

picking flint-flakes
of ash from her
nappy-ass hair

The collection's title echoes the Roman poet Juvenal's warning that fed and distracted populations can be more easily suppressed than the bored and starving. Matthews tackles contemporary iterations of these palliatives: from shopping malls and McDonald's to trap houses and rent subsidies paid directly to landlords. Stirring up De Bord's theory that our belongings and image can possess us, 'The Cost of the Floss' calls out the modern compulsion to share seductive images of luxury in hard times, as a woman discontentedly sits in an otherwise empty apartment wearing "a gold rope chain and the freshest shelltoe Adidas".

Bread and Circus tracks the same four-part structure as John Coltrane's landmark devotional *A Love Supreme*. The jazz record documents the saxophonist's break free from addiction through an improvised dialogue with God. Matthews' hybrid poems are equally concerned with recovery. They seek salvation from the shackles of capitalism.

JO CLEMENT

SELECTOR'S COMMENT

AIREA D. MATTHEWS

As a black American, writing into my own fullness is a political imperative. History is all too often written by the victors, and the victors often don't look like me. This lack of representation leads to an unbearable sameness, a narrowing, an essentialization. When static depictions are accepted, no pressure is applied to tradition, stereotypes, or received histories. What is most at stake for my work is pressuring monolithic depictions, valuing invention, and embracing a nuanced identity. Poetic identity broadens as form expands. Possibility enters, and poems (and poets) are freed beyond stricture or expectation.

My most recent book *Bread and Circus* situates the archive as a ghost text, a haunted text with the voice of experience overriding the voice of theory. Told in four parts – Acknowledgment, Resolution, Pursuance, and Psalm – the book amalgamates spectral imaging, photography, and poetry to explore the social and economic realities of race and class in America. The concept took form after a research trip to the University of Edinburgh to study Adam Smith's archives and his magnum opus, *The Wealth of Nations*. As a former economics student, I found myself perplexed by Smith's theory of the invisible hand, which claims that self-interest is the key to optimal, equitable outcomes. This collection is an interrogation of my own life and offers proof that Smith's theory fails when people, themselves, become commodities.

In my practice, dialectics become an oppositional force that considers how disorder originates in order, return mimics cyclicity, and myth informs memory. I find parallel themes most interesting when they struggle with one another to forge adjacent meanings and, in their theoretical opposition, produce luminous discoveries around universal human concerns, such as: Who holds value and who does not? How do individual struggles, personal and political, appear to disappear? How does language construct or deconstruct to trouble our presumptions?

AIREA RECOMMENDS

Ama Codjoe, *The Bluest Nude* (Milkweed Books); Nandi Comer, *Tapping Out* (Triquarterly); Courtney Faye Taylor, *Concentrate* (Graywolf); Aricka Foreman, *Salt Body Shimmer* (Yes Yes Books); Vievee Francis, *The Shared World* (Northwestern University Press); francine j. harris, *Here's The Sweet Hand* (FSG); Carl Phillips, *Then The War* (FSG); Alison Powell, *The Art Of Perpetuation* (Black Lawrence Press); Patricia Smith, *Unshuttered* (Northwestern University Press); Arisa White, *Who's Your Daddy* (Augury Books).

CHOICE

7

SEVERANCE

200 years after Franklin signed
the Declaration of Independence
Amtrak purchased the crumbling stone
viaducts and decrepit bridges between
Boston and Washington. In five years
the federal government would surface
245 miles of track, lay 171,000 ties,
renew 2,868 joints, interlock
5,800 switch timbers and order 492
Amfleet cars including sixteen sleek
Metroliners like one of the two
housed at Trenton Rail Station
where the authorities found
my father in stuporous nod
while on the official clock.
Having decided several offers
of rehab enough, Amtrak severed
all contractual encumbrances.

It was 1977 when my father stumbled
from that station into a recession but
first into Pete Lorenzo's bar
to pilfer time through a bottle
then plot provision—
three square, four souls—
strategizing who to feed
to whom.

HAUNTING AXIOMS

Some ghosts don't know they're dead.
This is also true of the living.

Some ghosts feel trapped on earth.
This is also true of the living.

Some ghosts re-enact their past.
This is also true of the living.

Some ghosts regret what's behind.
This is also true for some living.

Some ghosts have not earned rest.
This is also true for some living.

Some ghosts never seem to forget.
This is not quite true for the living.

Some ghosts return to their wound.
This is always true of the living.

SELIMA HILL

Born in Hampstead in 1945 into a family of painters, Selima Hill studied at Cambridge and now lives on the Dorset coast. She is the author of twenty poetry collections. She won first prize in the 1988 Arvon Foundation / *Observer* International Poetry Competition and her 1997 collection *Violet* was shortlisted for the Forward Prize for the Best Poetry Collection, the T.S. Eliot Prize and the Whitbread Poetry Award. In 2001 *Bunny* won the Whitbread Poetry Award. Her recent collections include *People Who Like Meatballs* (2012), shortlisted for the Forward Prize for Best Collection; *The Sparkling Jewel of Naturism* (2014) and *Men Who Feed Pigeons* (2021). She was recently awarded The King's Gold Medal for Poetry.

WOMEN IN COMFORTABLE SHOES

BLOODAXE BOOKS | £12.99 | PBS PRICE £9.75

Women in Comfortable Shoes exemplifies Selima Hill's dogged dedication to the short poem. Following the tradition of Strickland Gillilan, several of this impressive collection's four hundred and fifty poems are stark couplets, leaving little room to hide. Hill's speakers are far from reticent, elbowing readers with indelicate observations:

> The wedding-dress is going *Don't ask me!*
> *I* don't know what she's doing either!

Such humour initially deflects from the sincere concerns about women's experiences that steer the eleven sequences in the book. In 'Fishface', an errant girl is fed cupcakes at a convent school to distract from unholy experiences that await "on the other side of the wall". Another daughter fears her formidable father, who, by day, casts uneasy glances at her beachwear and, at night, casts menacing shadows in her bedroom ('My Spanish Swim Suit').

These vulnerabilities remain constant across generations. Self-assured Vera at first "rages like a star", preferring how a book "throbs inside the body" to beautification's drudgery ('Reduced to a Quivering Jelly'). However, troubled by nightmares in which she "ends up on the floor / wriggling like an upside-down-goldfish", she denies herself pleasures and is beset with senility:

> Yesterday she didn't trust the doctor,
> today she doesn't trust her own solicitor,
> tomorrow she will trust everyone.

In a recent conversation with Emily Berry, Hill said, "bearing witness always sounds as if you're witnessing something rather terrible or dramatic, but I would like to think we could bear witness to the tiniest things". Surging with shrieks of pain and howls of laughter, these poems transform life's inevitable mundanities into the fizziest, memorable moments.

As a surreal sister, Leonora Carrington, wrote: "sentimentality is a form of fatigue". Trusting in that same dispassion is undoubtedly part of Hill's enduring appeal. At seventy-seven, she certainly shows no signs of stopping.

AN INTERVIEW WITH SELIMA HILL

Neil Astley: You've moved from *Men Who Feed Pigeons* to *Women in Comfortable Shoes.* Can you say something about that journey, which wasn't a progression as such, given that many of the sequences were written alongside one another.

Selima Hill: My friend M's dying words were: "If anyone uses that word 'journey' to me again, I'll throttle them!" Stanley Kunitz talks about art as finding meaning instead of just "moving on". So, more like dancing than a journey. Dancing to my own music. Music becoming silence, "until the silence inside me matches the silence that surrounds me" (Per Petterson, trans. Anne Born). Writing poetry, to me, is also like playing tennis – trying to keep the ball in the air.

NA: The first sequences of *Women in Comfortable Shoes* – like *The Magnitude of My Sublime Existence* – relate in various ways to female friendship, but this is drawn upon a lifetime later in some cases. Can you tell us more about that?

SH: I suppose you could say I write out of gratitude. Writing as "a desire to live more honestly through language". Michelle Zauner described her music as "conversations I wanted to have with people but couldn't". In my case, I have been "non-verbal" at times. Writing suits me because it seems to be closer to thinking than it is to speaking. To give a very big answer to a very restrained question, Yves Klein quotes Bachelard as saying (if only I had the original French – locate it, someone!):

> First there is nothing,
> then there is deep nothing,
> then there is blue depth.

Or is that Bachelard quoting Yves Klein? I don't think so, although it makes more sense to me that way round. I put "non-verbal" in quotes because it seems to me a misnomer. (I was, on the contrary, "hyperlexic".) At the time I was called "mute", but mutism, like catatonia, sounds weirdly old-fashioned now.

Writing fiction "is like remembering what never happened"(Siri Hustvedt). And poetry, even in the first person, is fiction, although we know that doesn't fool all the people all the time. (One sequence I wrote, I changed the gender of the protagonist and that has fooled everybody.) Someone said (I'm sorry, I have forgotten who) "we" (The writers? The insane?) "build our own castles in the air and live in them" and writing is the drawbridge. Or, in the words of Joan Didion, "the writer is always tricking the reader into listening to the dream".

RECOMMENDATION

Mother said *It's dog eat dog out there*
Men will come and peel back your skin.

MY MOTHER AND THE SHEEP

Once I came downstairs to find a sheep
standing in the kitchen
and my mother
offering the sheep
a ginger biscuit
and looking overjoyed
to have a sheep
suddenly arrive
in her kitchen,
it used to reappear,
I remember,
and fall asleep
in my mother's lap
and keep her nice and warm
while I was swimming.

Image: Ethan Leonard

MAJELLA KELLY

Majella Kelly is an award winning writer from County Galway in the West of Ireland. Her poetry has been widely published and anthologised. Her debut pamphlet *Hush* was published in 2020 by ignitionpress and ten of her poems were published by Carcanet in the *Brotherton Prize Anthology* with the University of Leeds. In 2019 she won the Strokestown International Poetry Competition. In 2018 she won the *Ambit* Poetry Prize and came second in the Gregory O'Donoghue International Poetry Prize. *The Speculations of Country People* is her first book. You can find out more about her at www.majellakelly.com.

THE SPECULATIONS OF COUNTRY PEOPLE

PENGUIN | £10.99 | PBS PRICE £8.25

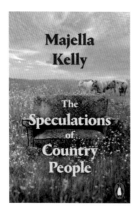

According to Merriam-Webster, the synonyms of speculate include cogitate, deliberate, reason, reflect and think. Split into four sections, this collection delivers all of these things. Majella Kelly begins with songs of longing for place. There's a beauty and invitation to paradise, there's a certain praise and chant in her first poem.

> I am from Kelly, Henebry, Burke, Scully.
> Hill. Mulligan. Cullinane...

The sonnet 'Cortege to Omey Island as Umbilical Cord' offers a lodestone for the collection – a haunting, a tethering to something buried, "its tidal waters keep breaking, pushing bones back up / from the sand swaddled in dandelions". Similarly 'Portrait of the City with Mastectomy' reveals a city harbouring something cancerous.

The second section 'Songeens for the Home Babies' excavates the horrors of the Tuam Mother and Baby Home where 796 children died between 1925 and 1961. Kelly bears witness to the voiceless, the vulnerable left in the hands of God. The blood of the innocent finds voice in the fields, crab apple trees and a hare, crying out from the ground. There is something chilling in the childhood warning:

> Be good, he was told,
> or you'll be put in with the Home Babies.

The sonnet 'Voice' left me in tears, each line to be read over and over again.

> To go into The Home was to be given
> your voice on a spoon and told: swallow it.

The volta truly hits home, as young women are silenced during childbirth:

> ...just to remind
> us we had sinned, the itchy hives of guilt
> distended, red and angry, in our bellies.

And yet salvation is found in the story of Julia Devaney who spent almost forty years in The Home. The third section of this book opens out into songs of such crystalline delicacy, for family and the people of the land. Kelly finishes with a rousing final section on love, a hymn of sensuous, salacious sweet poetry.

ROY McFARLANE

MAJELLA KELLY

My name is Majella Geraldine Kelly. I am called after my father's twin sisters, the youngest of ten siblings. They were called after Saint Gerard Majella, patron saint of expectant mothers. Catholic Ireland is quite firmly imprinted on my psyche. I was even what you might call a "good" Catholic up until the time I got divorced and was raising a child as a single parent.

I gradually realised that I was outside the house of the Church looking back in. I became drawn towards my Celtic pagan roots for some kind of spiritual solace to replace that thing I felt I had lost in a man-made religious organisation where I no longer felt welcome. The natural world, that the Pagans turned to, is a world of tremendous equality where gods and goddesses are equally revered. The poem 'Saint V Goddess' asks: which one would you like on your side on the worst day of your life?

I actually see many of the poems as my own little ode to sex in middle-age. I have finally shrugged off the guilt and the shame which has been so normalised for women in the Catholic Church. They would still like to deem me a "sinner", but these poems are me being unrepentant, and choosing joy over the threat of eternal damnation. I can find God in the taut body of a trout leaping upwards against a fast-flowing waterfall; or in the orgasm of the poem 'Hymn': "Oh God, Oh God, Oh God!". My church is now anywhere near a body of water. It flows through this collection. Spending time near water feeds that spiritual part of me that remains strong.

> Now I am a lake. A woman bends over me,
> Searching my reaches for what she really is.
>
> – Sylvia Plath

MAJELLA RECOMMENDS

Ed. Jeremy Noel-Tod, *The Penguin Book of The Prose Poem*; Alice Oswald, *The Thing in The Gap Stone Stile* (Faber); Natalie Diaz, *Postcolonial Love Poem* (Faber); Ada Limon, *The Carrying* (Milkweed Editions); Katharine Towers, *The Remedies* (Picador); Denise Riley, *Say Something Back* (Picador); Jack Underwood, *Happiness* (Faber); Caroline Bird, *In These Days of Prohibition* (Carcanet); John Burnside, *Black Cat Bone* (Cape); Anne Carson, *Autobiography of Red* (Cape); Alycia Pirmohamed, *Another Way to Split Water* (Polygon); Maggie Nelson, *Bluets* (Cape); Maurice Riordan, *The Water Stealer* (Faber).

RECOMMENDATION

Watch me set my every leaf ablaze

OVER-PAINTING

In the same way that Rudolph II
had the babies in Bruegel's *Massacre
of the Innocents* over-painted, so men
from Galway County Council were sent
with spades and grass seeds to lay a lawn
over the septic tank where juvenile
human remains were known to be found.

In the same way the nuns kept insisting
that no children were ever so buried.

In the painting a woman weeps over
an array of cheese and charcuterie,
which creates a scene arguably more
resonant of calculated evil;
the absence of blood and gore more eerie
and still than the heinous original.

LISA KELLY

Lisa Kelly has single-sided deafness. Her debut *A Map Towards Fluency* (2019) was shortlisted for the Michael Murphy Memorial Poetry Prize in 2021. She is co-Chair of *Magma* Poetry and a regular host of poetry evenings in London. She has been studying British Sign Language (BSL) for several years and has a Signature Level 6 qualification. Her poems have been selected for anthologies, including *Stairs and Whispers: D/deaf and Disabled Poets Write Back* (Nine Arches Press) and the *Forward Book of Poetry*. In 2021, she co-edited *What Meets the Eye*, an anthology of poetry and short fiction by UK Deaf, deaf and Hard of Hearing writers for Arachne Press. She teaches poetry and performance, and is a freelance technology journalist. She is also half Danish.

THE HOUSE OF THE INTERPRETER

CARCANET | £12.99 | PBS PRICE £9.75

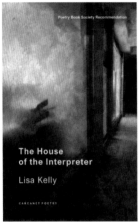

With poems as silken as truffle oil, *The House of the Interpreter* gathers embodied D/deaf experiences. Just as the middle ear has three bones, Lisa Kelly's second collection contains three striking sequences: 'Chamber', 'Oval Window' and 'Canal'. Here, buttercups bloom on the skin and fleshy mushrooms flicker into view like old movies. We encounter one bioluminescent agaric in the "Wood Wide Web" where:

> Tonight, we are not speaking,
> we are listening with our eyes.
> We feel for the forest as a ghost fungus might.

Responding to lines by Alexander Graham Bell – originator of damaging "visible speech" teachings – the long poem 'Researches in Electric Telephony' exposes how D/deaf people continue to be failed by the priorities of the hearing. It finds a fitting system in its "coupling" form, recently invented by Karen McCarthy Woolf:

> It is well known that deaf mutes are dumb
> *well known such terms must be undone*
>
> merely because they are deaf
> *clearly offensive to the Deaf*

Despite oralism's damaging restraints, these poems flourish, possessing and giving language to a quietude that is kindred to Raymond Antrobus' "sound of light"(*All the Names Given*). This line encourages us to consider how a person's first language might not be sound. Kelly is also an astonishing and noteworthy performer. Her synesthetic and sensorial poems vibrate with tongue pops and gripping British Sign Language gestures in complete tune with the physical and sonic rhythms at the beating heart of the visual vernacular form.

Bounteous and lush, *The House of the Interpreter* explores her transmutable mushroom motif both as a noun and verb. The result is a new D/deaf mode that spores fruitfully from the page into memory. Her poems remind us, as Ilya Kaminsky once said, that the D/deaf "don't believe in silence. Silence is the invention of the hearing".

SELECTOR'S COMMENT

JO CLEMENT

LISA KELLY

There is a vast spectrum about what it means to be D/deaf, but my deafness is the catalyst for exploring possibilities. It set me on the journey to learning British Sign Language, but inevitably the history of audism, and the stain of the ban on sign language at the Second International Congress on Education of the Deaf in 1880, looms large. In *The House of the Interpreter*, poems in the first section 'Chamber' were inspired by research into Deaf history, personal experience, and societal and political failings, as well as my time working as a communication support worker with a Deaf colleague in a supermarket in north London.

The dangers of monolingualism and monocultures, and their links to fascism find their objective correlative in the section 'Oval Window' through which fungi and mushrooms signal their magic; diversity; and potential. Despite their phenomenal ability as communicators and connectors – forming an essential part of the Wood Wide Web – fungi are often misunderstood and mycophobia is a theme which finds parallels in ignorance about perceptions of "other". Many poems were written in lockdown when searching for fungi deepened my appreciation of my deafness and the different ways we connect.

I aimed for a sense of "flow" in the final section 'Canal' featuring poems concerned with relations, visual art, and collective grief about the environment. From a societal and eco-poetic perspective, I hope the collection speaks for diversity and connectivity as the foundation for survival. I return to Merlin Sheldrake's proposition in his book *Entangled Life*, which inspired a golden shovel poem: "Might we be able to expand some of our concepts, such as speaking might not always require ears, and interpreting might not always require a nervous system? Are we able to do this without smothering other life forms with prejudice and innuendo?"

LISA RECOMMENDS

Jason Allen-Paisant, *Thinking with Trees* (Carcanet); Raymond Antrobus, *All The Names Given* (Picador); Khairani Barokka, *Ultimatum Orangutan* (Nine Arches Press); Julian Bishop, *We Saw It All Happen* (Fly On The Wall); Inger Christensen, *alphabet* (Bloodaxe); Ilya Kaminsky, *Deaf Republic* (Faber); Safiya Kamaria Kinshasa, *Cane, Corn & Gully* (Out-Spoken); Lucy Mercer, *Emblem* (Prototype); Pascale Petit, *Mama Amazonica* (Bloodaxe); Stav Poleg, *The City* (Carcanet); Laura Scott, *The Fourth Sister* (Carcanet); Daniel Sluman, *Single Window* (Nine Arches Press); D.L. Williams, *Interdimensional Traveller* (Burning Eye Books).

In the House of the Interpreter,
consonants are lost and dropped letters litter the floor.

#WHEREISTHEINTERPRETER

It is always an access issue, always a case of make do,
make do with subtitles, make do with delay,
catch up because you don't matter and are relatively few.

The Prime Minister briefs on the pandemic every day,
what we should do because 'we are all in this together'
but 87,000 people cannot hear what he has to say.

In Scotland and Wales, they provide an interpreter
for vital information about how the virus is spreading,
what is expected of us, which problems might occur

if we don't understand exactly where we're heading,
if we don't stand united and follow government guidelines.
If your first language is sign, if you have no hearing

then hear this: the Deaf community should not be side-lined.
Give equal access to information for all. *We, the undersigned.*

I LISA KELLY

ADAM LOWE

Adam Lowe is the UK's LGBT+ History Month Poet Laureate and was Yorkshire's Olympic Poet for 2012. Born in Leeds, he lives in Manchester. Adam has worked with The Poetry School, the University of Leeds, the University of Central Lancashire and English PEN. He was named one of the 20 Best Writers under 40 in Leeds for the LS13 Awards and his chapbook *Precocious* was nominated for the *Guardian* First Book Prize. He was a finalist for the Venture, Eric Hoffer, Lambda Literary and Live Canon Awards, and is a fellow of The Complete Works and Obsidian Foundation.

PATTERFLASH

PEEPAL TREE PRESS | £9.99 | PBS PRICE £7.50

In 'Maroon in Blonde' we see a young child holding the attention of his father's drinking buddies with stories, similarly Adam Lowe loves to usurp a narrative, tell his story, wicked and full of resistance, holding you in the palm of his hands entranced by his lyrics.

Patter flash –
gossip, chat, ostentations or pretentious speech; the lyrics pouring out of my gob.

In 'A Glossary of Polari', Lowe takes the weight of language and gives us a key into the community and stories told in this collection. He takes us on a wild unapologetic journey, a shibboleth for the reader to be granted access behind closed doors, into another world.

From 'Downlow Download', with its sharp staccato and furtive rendering, to 'Elsie Tanner for Teens', full of enjambments, these poems are liberating. The speaker will not be held by your gaze or ideas of morality. 'Elegy For The Latter-Day Teen Wilderness Years' pulls back the covers on what was once clandestine and covert:

> We lived in the witching, hybrid hours, where the dark and dim had
>   pride of place.
> We were bold and wild, our songs ricocheted against the naked heavens.
>
> Then the clouds would thicken like stones, and we retreat; the morning
> pouring over us like molten gold, swallowing the glitter and bruises of night.

These lines encapsulate the ever-presence of danger, the sense of living in the margins with no regrets, the saccharine and sacred play on sex and desire.

Discussing literary language and traditions, the black gay Bronx poet Reginald Shepherd once said, "I wrestle with this necessary angel and rise renamed, blessed but also lamed." Whether the speaker in *Patterflash* is Beyoncé, re-writing the gospel, engaging with Norman MacCaig or bearing witness to the souls lost in the Middle Passage or Hamza Ali Al-Khateeb, everyone rises, renamed, blessed and gloriously, beautifully, lamed.

SELECTOR'S COMMENT

ADAM LOWE

In *Patterflash*, I tried to capture the voices of some of the key personages in my life whose stories changed me and whose words I can still hear today. Take 'Gingerella's Date', which started out in my voice but only really began to soar when I channelled an old friend from my days in Leeds. Take, also, 'Vada That', which bounces along with the cadence of a certain cackling sister of mine with whom I've shared many a story and many a bevvy down on Canal Street. By focussing the stories I wanted to tell through the voices of those people who have changed me, I hope to enact a little bit of that same change on the reader.

There was a temptation, at one point, to fill the book with poems in Polari. I quickly realised the folly in that. Frankly, the vividness and vitality of the language isn't reflected in the volume of words it offers – even throwing in my own neologisms, 538 words (give or take) is a paltry "language" from which to write a book. I wanted to preserve that language, as much as I could, but also keep it alive. Because Polari has refused to die out, and it has changed. I also didn't want to suffocate the book with endless poems where I euphemistically tip the brandy. So I decided, instead, to explore the same ecstasies of language throughout the breadth of those changemaking voices I still hear. The voices I summon are Tyke and Scouse, arch and earthy, sleazy and beautiful. They remain as a personal, private chorus I can draw upon to guide me to the right phrase, the right idea, the right response... That's why Manchester's street lingo gets fluffed up by American ballroom culture, and why Biblical melodrama is tarted up with classic camp.

Importantly, I hoped that by sharing these voices, I could allow others to experience their mouthfeel and their aftertaste. There are stories of those who may be forgotten or ignored, and those who may be remembered but maligned. I hope you get even a small taste of the meaning they gave me, but I also hope I have done them justice with that old patter flash.

ADAM RECOMMENDS ——————————————————

Afshan D'souza-Lodhi, *re:desire* (Burning Eye); Patience Agbabi, *Bloodshot Monochrome* (Canongate); Andrew McMillan, *physical* (Jonathan Cape); Jay Bernard, *Surge* (Vintage); Dorothea Smartt, *Reader, I Married Him & Other Queer Goings-On* (Peepal Tree Press); Dean Atta, *There is (still) love here* (Nine Arches); Shivanee Ramlochan, *Everyone Knows I Am a Haunting* (Peepal Tree Press); Warsan Shire, *teaching my mother how to give birth* (flipped eye); Rommi Smith, *Poems from Mornings & Midnights* (Peepal Tree Press); Maz Hedgehog, *The Body in Its Seasons* (Burning Eye).

I RECOMMENDATION

Descend with me into a bruise-lit underworld

Image: Lee Baxter

THE MARRIAGE

In the shade we fold into bows of limbs,
our shadows pool among roots. You succumb,
pull from the branch low-slung bulbs of delight.
Your knife orbits the golden fruit, disrobes
its pithy sunlight. You give it to me:
a half-moon, a bowl of amethysts.
This dowry in your fist illuminates;
the canopy of the blossoming tree
becomes sanctuary no more, reveals
flesh in dark ridges, wet, scattered with seeds.
I am anointed with juice that beads and runs free.
You feed me morsels like purple stars. Fill
the groove of my collarbone. You dress me in
this sap necklace. Make me your shining queen.

THE EDITORS

Vidyan Ravinthiran was born in Leeds, to Sri Lankan Tamils. His debut *Grun-tu-molani* (Bloodaxe, 2014) was shortlisted for the Forward Prize for Best First Collection, the Seamus Heaney Centre Poetry Prize and the Michael Murphy Memorial Prize. *The Million-petalled Flower of Being Here* (Bloodaxe, 2019) was shortlisted for the Forward Prize, the T.S. Eliot Prize and Ledbury Munthe Poetry Prize. After posts at Cambridge, Durham and Birmingham, he now teaches at Harvard University.

Seni Seneviratne is a writer of English and Sri Lankan heritage published by Peepal Tree Press. Her books include *Wild Cinnamon* and *Winter Skin* (2007), *The Heart of It* (2012), and *Unknown Soldier* (2019), which was a Poetry Book Society Recommendation and highly commended in the Forward Poetry Prizes. She is currently working on an LGBTQ project with Sheffield Museums entitled *Queering the Archive*. She lives in Matlock.

Shash Trevett is a Tamil from Sri Lanka who came to the UK to escape the civil war. She is a poet and a translator of Tamil poetry into English. Her pamphlet *From a Borrowed Land* was published in 2021 by Smith / Doorstop. She has been on the judging panel for the PEN Translates awards and was a Visible Communities Translator in Residence at the National Centre for Writing. She is a Ledbury Critic and a Board Member of *Modern Poetry in Translation*. She lives in York.

OUT OF SRI LANKA

BLOODAXE BOOKS | £14.99 | PBS PRICE £11.25

A. Sivanandan, the Sri Lankan, anti-racist activist and writer, once said "we are here because you were with us". It is important to start at that point. Sri Lanka, a place often sold as a vision of golden beaches and swaying palm trees, began as a people colonised by the Portuguese, Dutch and British. Out of this fracture, Ravinthiran, Seneviratne and Trevett have gathered together over a hundred poets into an anthology of writing in English or translated from Tamil and Sinhala, writing from a diaspora that has fault lines stretching across the globe.

Liyanage Amarakeerthi calls for 'A Poem's Plea': "In that minute space between Us and Them; *there* allow me to *be*." These poems occupy that space between the intimate and the epic, between civil war and environmental disasters, dissent and divide. They conjure a sky big enough to cover all the possibilities of being Sri Lankan, a sky that holds the past and present.

> Behold as this crazy woman you rejected
> Conjures up
> an entire sky

This is a collection of roots and being uprooted. Ruwan Bandujeewa's poem 'Earthworms' offers advice to an earthworm's son to stay underground during a ploughing festival and these proverbs are sprinkled throughout this anthology.

In the poem 'Lavannya's Twilight Bike Ride', Suresh Canagarajah illuminates the horrors of war, bearing witness to atrocities and humanity, in ways both cinematic and poetic. The poet Cheran urges us not to forget; haunted by dead bodies, an upturned burnt-out car, a fragment of a sari:

> how shall I forget the broken shards
> and the scattered rice
> laying parched upon the Earth.

There are angry waves crashing throughout this collection, the reverberations of colonialism and imperialism, swelled into a civil war, factions and the demonising of Muslim communities, yet amid all of this, each poem is a silent dewdrop shining on the Sri Lankan diaspora. A compilation of jasmine in full bloom and honey birds by day.

UNHEEDED SIGHTS
BY AALIYAAL

After the rains
the tiled roofs shone
sparkling clean.
The sky was not yet minded
to become a deeper blue.
The tar roads reminded me
intermittently of rainbows.
From the entire surface of the earth
a fine smoke arose
like the smoke of frankincense, or akil wood,
the earth's scent stroking the nostrils,
fragrant as a melody.

As the army truck coming towards me
drives away,
a little girl transfers her candy-floss
from one hand to the other
raises her right hand up high
and waves her tiny fingers.

And like the sweet surprise
of an answering air-letter
all the soldiers standing in the truck
wave their hands, exactly like her.

The blood that froze in my veins
for an instant, in amazement,
flows again rapidly, asking aloud,
"War? In this land?
Who told you?"

Translated from Tamil by Lakshmi Holmström

LASDAIR MAC MHAIGHSTIR ALASDAIR

TAYLOR STRICKLAND

Alasdair Mac Mhaighstir Alasdair (c.1698-c.1770) was a Scottish Gaelic poet, lexicographer, military officer, and Gaelic language tutor to Charles Edward Stuart, popularly known as Bonnie Prince Charlie. Little of his life is confirmed aside from his role as a teacher and as a captain in the 1745 rebellion. He compiled and published the first Gaelic-English dictionary and his only volume of poetry *Aiseirigh na Seann Chànain Albannach* (1751) was the first secular work to be published in a Celtic language. His reputation stirred controversy and his book was reputedly burnt in Edinburgh after publication.

Taylor Strickland is a poet and translator from the US. He is the author of *Commonplace Book* and *Dastram / Delirium*. His poem 'The Low Road' was adapted by the American composer Andrew Kohn and performed in Orkney. His poem 'Nine Whales, Tiree' is in the process of being adapted with filmmaker Olivia Booker and composer Fee Blumenthaler. He is a doctoral candidate in literary translation at the University of Glasgow.

DASTRAM / DELIRIUM
ALASDAIR MAC MHAIGHSTIR ALASDAIR
BROKEN SLEEP BOOKS | £10.99 | PBS PRICE £8.25

Poetry Book Society Translation Choice

**Dastram /
Delirium**

Selected Poems of
Alasdair mac Mhaighstir Alasdair
Versions by
Taylor Strickland

A necessary commonplace of translator's notes is that all such work is, as Taylor Strickland puts it, "improper representation". The best poets are specific to their language, the meaning of their music essentially untranslatable. Instead, translators engage in techniques that are at their best subversive, doing "wrong in order to do right".

Alasdair Mac Mhaighstir Alasdair (known as MacDhòmhnaill in Gaelic) is one of the most significant poets in the history of Scottish literature. His *Aiseirigh na Seann Chànain Albannach* (*The Resurrection of the Old Scots Language*) was the first volume of original verse to be published in Scottish Gaelic. It is easy to draw parallels to Scotland's other 18th century linguistic resurrection man, Robert Burns, but MacDhòmhnaill, as a war poet, Jacobite officer and tutor to Charles Edward Stuart was by far the more politically influential in his time. That so few readers now are familiar with his verse is one indication of the persecution and continuing marginalisation of Gaelic literature in these islands.

Strickland's method, then, is not to replicate the deep patterning and punning of the original Gaelic, but to lead the reader into the original through an English which is sharp, playful, questioning and peculiar. The selection shifts easily, as does MacDhòmhnaill's body of work, between the sublime and the insalubrious, between praise and condemnation. Much of *Dastram* is drawn from the poems to Mòrag, with a frank eroticism that is both refreshing and troubling. Each word of the translation carries its weight well, and the challenge of bringing a fresh perspective to a much-interpreted poet, of making his work anew for a contemporary audience, is well met.

Christopher Whyte's influential polemic *Against Self-Translation* comments that some English versions act "like grimly haunting doubles from which Gaelic poems no longer have any hope of being prised". *Dastram* unknots this problem through a wilful, delightful multiplication of meaning that is deeply in service to the original. If the brevity of the collection leaves the reader, like Alasdair for Mòrag, demanding more, then it is to the good that there are many hundreds more lines and centuries of Gaelic translation still left to pursue.

HARRY JOSEPHINE GILES

SIUBHAL

Delirium! Delirium
from her, a girl blonde,
lurid: how she snuffs out
her own flint-spark glow,
and in one white bite
hewn from snow.
As sex and excess,
as body and beauty,
so Dido, so Venus,
so Mòrag ravishes
my seasons,
my genius
spent.
A girl with sharp agency
can pierce the heart
clean through.

O dastram, dastram,
Dastram Mòrag!
Rìbhinn bhuidh', bhasdalach,
Leac-ruiteach ròsach;
A gruaidhean air lasadh
Mar an lasair-chlach dhathte,
'S a deud mar a' sneachda,
Cruinn-shnaighte'n dlùth òrdugh;
Ri Venus cho tlachgmhor
An taitneachdainn fheòlmhor
Ri Dido cho maiseach,
Cho snasmhor's cho còrr rith';
'S e thionnsgain dhomh caitheamh
'S a lùghdaich mo ràithean,
A' bhallag ghrinn laghach
Chuir na gathan sa'm fheòil-sa.

KAREN DOWNS-BARTON

Karen Downs-Barton is an Anglo-Romani writer who, after a peripatetic childhood, including times in state care, now lives in Wiltshire. Winner of the 2021 Cosmo Davenport-Hines prize and a 2022 Creative Future silver medallist, she is a PhD candidate at King's College London, exploring identity through minority languages and multilingualism in entertainment industries.

DIDICOY BY KAREN DOWNS-BARTON

SMITH | DOORSTOP | £6.00 |

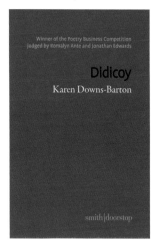

What does it mean to be both an outsider and also a part of a community? *Didicoy* dwells in this in-between space where languages, homes and memories seep into each other. Several poems document growing up in state care, using fragmented forms to piece together (and pull apart) memories of displacement. But tenderness and closeness are also at the core of these poems, many of which are vivid portraits of motherhood and sisterhood.

> my Romani tongue, a wayside patrin
> of twigs and leaves

In a series of powerful multilingual poems, English and Romani are threaded together in rhyme and rhythm. This shifting linguistic field is like a woven landscape, as metaphors of weaving often come into play. 'A Confluence of Red and Silks' is diaphanous and slippery in texture, as it shifts between memories, between English and Romani.

The poems delight in bodily textures and scents, brimming with heat and hunger. In 'A Love of Flesh', a childhood meal is rendered in rich detail, somehow both visceral and tender. Many poems conjure these hidden spaces you want to "climb inside", as the poet writes in a brilliant sequence titled 'Dear Faye' where the prose poem form becomes a kind of memory room or a spell of protection. A secret space where a scene of warmth has been preserved on the page, kept safe.

In the final 'Dear Faye' poem, which stands out in the collection, there's an uneasy sense of shapeshifting. This otherworldly poem is like a tethering, a grasping, or a spell "to fix the seep of your wandering outline." Some kind of haunting – a bright energy, not one of overwhelming darkness – runs under the surface which we can feel but cannot quite touch. With this threading together of languages comes a sense of stillness and a final image of mending:

> I'll mend myself with
> a red ribbon, write myself free with an alchemy of oak galls, crushed
> eggshells, Gum Arabic and dripped
>   honey.

ARJI MANUELPILLAI & NINA MINGYA POWLES

MI LOKI GILI:
MY SONG OF LIFE

I practice the language my grandparents forgot
in a van, my *vardo*, parked in an *atchin tan* –
a layby far from fields, my off-grid home.
When the *gorja* retreated to their brick houses,
I lost the stigma of being an outsider.
In the hush, I only heard songbirds.
The city paused for the longest moment,
its soul grew calmer, the air grew cleaner,
and I stopped running just to stop looking backward.

I learned new words, limos : acceptance, smirom : peace.

To stop looking backward I just stopped running and
my soul grew calmer as the air grew cleaner.
For the longest moment, the city paused;
in the hush, I only heard songbirds.
I lost the stigma of being an outsider,
retreated from the *gorja* in their brick houses.
I lay by fields, my off-grid home, a Rom, far
in an *atchin tan*. In a parked van, my *vardo,*
I practice the language my grandparents forgot.

Vardo: home, wagon, caravan
Atchin tan: stopping place, safe place to stay
Gorja: non-gypsy.

KAREN DOWNS-BARTON

SUMMER BOOK REVIEWS

Spanning over ten years of writing, this collection showcases CAConrad's long trajectory of crafting poems that are effortlessly chameleonic, supernaturally visceral, and fiercely attentive to ecological and social concerns. In CAConrad's vision nothing escapes poetic entanglement; everything is poetry, "but I can put every poem / I ever wrote / in a pile / and burn / them". These vital poems reveal the urgency for connection with our bodies, our planet, and our words.

MAY | PENGUIN | £12.99 | PBS PRICE £9.75

Neptune's Projects repurposes mythology to imagine a god, once "all-powerful and unopposed", now adrift in a world threatened with loss and extinction. The poetic voice remains wry and hopeful; melancholic and playful, perched between fury and fun as it considers the fate of humanity under the present day climate crisis. Daring in both subject matter, poetic and linguistic form, *Neptune's Projects* combines themes of expectation and disappointment to thrilling effect.

APRIL | NINE ARCHES PRESS | £10.99 | PBS PRICE £8.25

There is such quiet understanding in this collection about a woman's journey from childhood to death. Poems about domestic violence, Jewishness and queerness explore the hidden spaces behind words and everyday life. Playfulness and poignancy cohabit: a witty poem on antisemitism ("our nose grows / with the lies you tell about us") is followed by one about exile from Odessa. Old age, with its "grip-slip subsidence" is finally the time when life says, "let's make friends".

APRIL | SEREN BOOKS | £9.99 | PBS PRICE £7.50

LEDBURY CRITICS TAKEOVER

ROWAN
EVANS

A Method,
A Path

"Where's the short-wave radio, / the meat sandwich, the bag of wood?" Evans writes dispatches from a far country, where the English is Old, where the textures of life are an uncanny translation of our own political and existential divisions. Everything feels unnaturally parsed into absence or something it ought not to be, "birds already hidden in etymology as a forest" and "yr house" is "a pastime between two / empires of toadflax". Evans knows that language can soothe and inflame.

JUNE | BLOOMSBURY | £9.99 | PBS PRICE £7.50

Fletcher's poems slip down as easily as "the gin stinging my teeth," as "little wet bites of things we cannot say". Female rage takes many forms in these poems, moving sharply down the lines, as much a cry as a warning: "bark, bark, I said to strangers, / instead of: get me help, / get me the fuck out of this place. / I do not think that I will live / another seven years." *Plus ultra*, go beyond – the everyday, class, gender and pain – Fletcher urges us.

APRIL | CHEERIO | £11.00 | PBS PRICE £8.25

Earth House
Matthew Hollis

Matthew Hollis's second collection blends the human and the natural in novel ways: "you steady the wheel, reminded of your place, / and look down on the scarp with its paper-/ clip turns." Hollis makes deft use of rhythm and rhyme: "The brim that broke the river came on land. / Its skirts were vast from so much rain and made / the grass beneath it dance, wild hair of the drowned." The result is a sweeping meditation on time, history, and our place in the natural world.

APRIL | BLOODAXE BOOKS | £14.99 | PBS PRICE £11.25

| BOOK REVIEWS

MEENA KANDASAMY: TOMORROW SOMEONE WILL ARREST YOU
REVIEWED BY LEAH JUN OH

Joyfully rendering the indirect ineffective, "THE POET" beguilingly declares to her language: "Here, the only rule: / What you see is what you say – / Nothing seen goes unsaid." Meena Kandasamy's lines of poetry cascade in an unstoppable poetic-surging into a rallying cry that denounces the injustices of caste and gender and right-wing state terror to reinvigorate those who "struggle & think & love together with THE POET".

Meena Kandasamy

MAY | ATLANTIC POETRY | £10.99 | PBS PRICE £8.25

NICK LAIRD: UP LATE
REVIEWED BY OLUWASEUN S. OLAYIWOLA

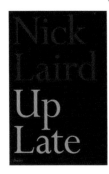

Up Late focalises around the death of the poet's father. "But I know what the body wants. / Continuance. Continuance. Continuance / at any cost." Foregrounded against the Pandemic, here is a poet in outcry, chiefly questioning how – amidst "consciousness['s]... white noise" – one can remain present. "When a thought comes that will lead you / into the past or future, dismiss it", the poet writes, in this elegiac collection which forces a smile in the wake of familial grief.

JUNE | FABER | £14.99 | PBS PRICE £11.25

NESS OWEN: MOON JELLYFISH CAN BARELY SWIM
REVIEWED BY MAGGIE WANG

Ness Owen's collection has all the fluidity of the ocean upon which it builds its world. Just as the titular moon jellyfish "have no choice but to go where the ocean takes them", these poems move smoothly between "the wind-whipped / waves where the / drowned return and / skylines rise and fall." Though the book begins at sea, its conversational yet lush language lends itself to a broader focus encompassing the speaker's own life, as well as Welsh politics and identity.

APRIL | PARTHIAN BOOKS | £10.00 | PBS PRICE £7.50

AL-SADDIQ AL-RADDI: A FRIEND'S KITCHEN
TRANS. BRYAR BAJALAN & SHOOK
REVIEWED BY SHALINI SENGUPTA

Bajalan and Shook's translations of the exiled Sudanese poet Al-Raddi contain tender poems marking absence and the melancholy of exile, "a cup of coffee less warm / Than your kiss at my goodbye". Written in London during the 2019 uprisings against Omar al-Bashir, these poems began as a stream of consciousness steeped in allusion and mysticism. This is a fantastic translation of a poet in disconnection, living "on a slight thread of aroma" from back home.

JUNE | PTC | £9.00 | PBS PRICE £6.75

KAE TEMPEST: DIVISIBLE BY ITSELF AND ONE
REVIEWED BY SHALINI SENGUPTA

Tempest's new book resonates with a fierce grace and finds the perfect balance between their public-facing performance and a more contemplative voice. Questions of integrity and form – both human and mathematical, like the prime number of the title – are central. Tempest chronicles the human body's limits and captures the tension between self and collective. This is a powerful act of self-affirmation: a poignant document that is both introspective and prophetic.

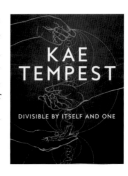

APRIL | PICADOR | £10.99 | PBS PRICE £8.25

ALLY ZLATAR: THE MONSTERS ARE ALIVE
REVIEWED BY LEAH JUN OH

Accompanied by paintings of fashionably dressed monsters posing boldly, styled in magazine model spreads, the poems careen between sincere melodrama, grand declarations, and lurid rhymes caught in the intensity of feeling absolute despair: "my beaches stand still waiting / for your waves of validation / what a hopeless fixation". Sontag says "In naïve, or pure, Camp, the essential element is seriousness, a seriousness that fails." I'm unnerved that "my bomb shelter is weak and filled with my shrieks" is kind of fun.

APRIL | GOOD PRESS | £8.99 | PBS PRICE £6.75

| BOOK REVIEWS

SUMMER PAMPHLETS

WILLIAM GEE: TRUST FALL

William Gee entrusts us with a glimpse into the psycho-geography of chronic illness, as he navigates life with a "sickness (which) eats up every space for you". These poems are underpinned by bodily alienation, "*his* body... *I* sit / inside of *him* like a church", but Gee moves beyond bodily constraints to forge a soaring lyric which transcends "this always ill". Between the sudden joy of a good day and the redemptive power of love, the poet learns to trust the body in free fall and accept the lyricism of "letting go".

OUT-SPOKEN   PRESS | £8.00 |

TRUST FALL

WILLIAM GEE

JOHN GOODBY: SO, RISE

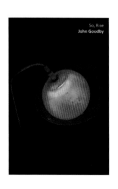

So, Rise
John Goodby

This final part of Goodby's chapbook trilogy, disorientates and questions, "Why here? I build an upside down Day". Rising out of fragments of existing poems, OuLiPo-style, these are upturned poems, full of internal echoes and united by an experimental revelry in the sounds and textures of words. Systematic and cosmic in scope, *So, Rise* glimpses the world as if through a kaleidoscope, cut up and coalescing back into being. These poems skilfully reflect the alienation of illness and the resurrection of recovery. So, rise.

RED   CEILINGS   PRESS | £8.00 |

SIMON MADDRELL: ISLE OF SIN

In *Isle of Sin*, Maddrell thrashes out and rehashes the queer history of the Isle of Man, swinging from heart-wrenching poems with gut-punch endings ('I Could Have Been You') to wry, dry satire ('Bona Vacantia'). With the first half dedicated to the life of Dursley McLinden, who inspired the character of Ritchie in Channel 4's *It's A Sin*, and the second covering the fight for queer rights on the Isle of Man, this is a revelatory and impactful work.

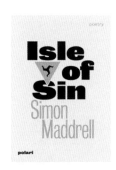

Isle of Sin
Simon Maddrell
polari

POLARI   PRESS | £9.99 |

KIRSTIE MILLAR: THE STRANGE EGG

A Gothic allegory for the experience of endometriosis, *The Strange Egg* is a beautiful, visceral, sometimes terrifying prose-poem which reads like a dark fairy tale. Inextricably linking the human body with the animal and casting medical professionals as uncanny tormentors, this work is a compelling expression of gendered illness and pain. Part of The Emma Press Art Squares series, this collectable pamphlet features striking illustrations by Hannah Mumby.

THE   EMMA   PRESS | £10.00 |

BETHANY MITCHELL: SHINGLE

This astounding pamphlet-length poem conjures the landscape of the north Norfolk coast, using language which is vital and immediate. The accumulation of life and language builds a sense of place around the observer, even to the point of her almost-erasure; an act which questions how we might write the human out of ecopoetry entirely, and whether or not we should: "the opposable thumb / works the scissors / + untangles what need not be untangled // can we stay tangled for a while   please".

BROKEN   SLEEP   BOOKS | £7.99 |

ZOË WALKINGTON: I HATE TO BE THE ONE TO TELL YOU THIS

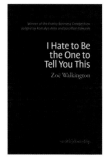

There is something deeply comic and yet disconcerting about this Poetry Business prize-winning debut. Beneath the hilarity lies a latent sense of threat and, to misquote, deniable plausibility: "It wasn't raining, and I was safe / in the knowledge I didn't exist." In Walkington's world "the dog has taken to offering unsolicited advice", infidelity and lies abound, and perilous bridges are the place to find love. This is a riotous and truly irresistible pamphlet.

SMITH | DOORSTOP | £6.50 |

SUMMER BOOK LISTINGS

Sam Adams	Letters from Wales...	Parthian Books	£20.00
A.J. Akoto	Unmothered	Arachne Press	£9.99
Connor Allen	Miracles	Lucent Dreaming	£10.00
Cathleen Allyn Conway	Bloofer	Broken Sleep Books	£9.50
Annie Bachini	Two Haiku Poets	Iron Press	£7.00
Charlie Baylis	A Fondness for the Colour Green	Broken Sleep Books	£9.99
Julia Bell	Hymnal	Parthian Books	£10.00
Robert Best	Into the Wolf	Iron Press	£6.00
John Birtwhistle	Partial Shade: Poems New and Selected	Carcanet Press	£14.99
Julian Bishop	We Saw It All Happen	Fly on the Wall Press	£9.99
Tom Branfoot	This Is Not An Epiphany	The Poetry Business	£6.00
Dylan Brennan	Let the Dead	Banshee Press	£8.99
Zakia Carpenter-Hall	Into the Same Sound Twice	Seren	£6.00
Cat Chong	712 Stanza Homes for the Sun	Broken Sleep Books	£12.99
Jane Clarke	A Change in the Air	Bloodaxe Books	£10.99
Rachael Clyne	You'll Never Be Anyone Else	Seren	£9.99
Joey Connolly	The Recycling	Carcanet Press	£12.99
CAConrad	You Don't Have What It Takes to Be...	Penguin Press	£12.99
Fred d'Aguiar	Arboretum for the Hunted	Arc Publications	£8.00
Rishi Dastidar	Neptune's Projects	Nine Arches Press	£10.99
Melissa Davies	Arctic Diaries	Arachne Press	£9.99
Isobel Dixon	A Whistling of Birds	Nine Arches Press	£12.99
Maura Dooley	Five Fifty-Five	Bloodaxe Books	£10.99
Michael Edwards	Another Art of Poetry	Carcanet Press	£14.99
Rowan Evans	A Method, a Path	Bloomsbury	£9.99
Kit Fan	The Ink Cloud Reader	Carcanet Press	£12.99
Tristram Fane Saunders	Before We Go Any Further	Carcanet Press	£12.99
Katie Farris	Standing in the Forest of Being Alive	Pavilion Poetry Press	£10.99
Sarah Fletcher	PLUS ULTRA	Cheerio Publishing	£11.00
Michael Foley	The Whole Thing	Mica Press	£10.00
Rebecca Goss	Latch	Carcanet Press	£12.99
Jorie Graham	to 2040	Carcanet Press	£15.99
Ben Harker	Collected Poems of Montagu Slater	Smokestack Books	£8.99
Lesley Harrison	Kitchen Music	Carcanet Press	£12.99
Emily Hasler	Local Interest	Pavilion Poetry Press	£10.99
Selima Hill	Women in Comfortable Shoes	Bloodaxe Books	£12.99
Norbert Hirschhorn	Over the Edge	Holland Park Press	£10.00
Jodie Hollander	Nocturne	Pavilion Poetry Press	£10.99
Matthew Hollis	Earth House	Bloodaxe Books	£14.99
Rosie Jackson	Love Leans Over the Table	Two Rivers Press	£10.99
Emma Jeremy	sad thing angry	Out-Spoken Press	£11.99
Kris Johnson	Ghost River	Bloodaxe Books	£10.99
Meena Kandasamy	Tomorrow Someone Will Arrest You	Atlantic Books	£10.99
Bhanu Kapil	Incubation	Prototype Publishing	£12.00
Majella Kelly	The Speculations of Country People	Penguin Press	£10.99
Lisa Kelly	The House of the Interpreter	Carcanet Press	£12.99
Matthew Kinlin	Songs of Xanthina...	Broken Sleep Books	£9.99
Richard Knott	Selected Poems of Clive Branson	Smokestack Books	£8.99
Daniel Kramb	Little Estuaries	Het Moet-Menard Press	£10.99
Neetha Kunaratnam	Cauc/asian	Blue Diode Press	£10.00
Nick Laird	Up Late	Faber	£14.99
Vanessa Lampert	Say It With Me	Seren	£9.99
Adam Lowe	Patterflash	Peepal Tree Press	£9.99
Toby Martinez de las Rivas	Floodmeadow	Faber	£12.99